The Age of Destruction and Lies

By the Same Author

A Confusion of Marys [with Sarah Cave] (Shearsman Books 2020)
The Return of Doom-Headed Three [with Daniel Y Harris]
(Knives Forks & Spoons Press 2018)
Contextual Studies (Broken Sleep 2018)
The Co-ordinates of Doubt [with Daniel Y Harris]
(Knives Forks & Spoons Press 2017)
Dear Mary (Shearsman Books 2017)
Impossible Songs [with Sarah Cave] (Analogue Flashback 2017)
Love Songs for an Echo (Original Plus 2016)
Reasons (Hesterglock 2015)
The Return of the Man Who Has Everything (Shearsman Books 2015)
Esophagus Writ [with Daniel Y Harris] (Knives Forks and Spoons Press 2014)
Ballads of the Alone (Shearsman Books 2013)
Encouraging Signs. Interviews, essays and conversations (Shearsman Books 2013)
Tower of Babel (Like This Press 2013)
Leading Edge Control Technology (Knives Forks & Spoons Press 2013)
Voiceover (Riverine) [with Paul Sutton] (Knives Forks and Spoons Press 2012)
Wildlife (Shearsman Books 2011)
A Music Box of Snakes [with Peter Gillies] (Knives Forks and Spoons Press 2010)
The Fantasy Kid (Salt Publications 2010)
Boombox (Shearsman Books 2009)
Lost in the Slipstream (Original Plus 2009)
An Experiment in Navigation (Shearsman Books 2008)
Ex Catalogue (Shadow Train 2006)
A Conference of Voices (Shearsman Books 2004)
The Museum of Light (Arc Publications 2003)

As Editor:

Yesterday's Music Today [with Mike Ferguson]
(Knives Forks and Spoons Press 2015)
Smartarse (Knives Forks and Spoons Press 2011)
From Hepworth's Garden Out (Shearsman Books 2010)
Troubles Swapped for Something Fresh: manifestos and unmanifestos
(Salt Publications 2009)

Rupert M Loydell

The Age of Destruction and Lies

Shearsman Books

First published in the United Kingdom in 2023 by
Shearsman Books Ltd
PO Box 4239
Swindon
SN3 9FN

Shearsman Books Ltd Registered Office
30–31 St. James Place, Mangotsfield, Bristol BS16 9JB
(this address not for correspondence)

www.shearsman.com

ISBN 978-1-84861-889-3

Acknowledgements

The Alice One (Mid Life Crisis Zine Series, 2016), *Amethyst Review, Bomb Damage Maps* (The Red Ceilings Press, 2020), *Cholla Needles, Duane's Poetree, The Fortnightly Review, The Gospel According to Archbishop Makeshift* (Analogue Flashback Books, 2016), *Gravy from the Gazebo, I Am Not A Silent Poet, International Times, Literature Today, Local Nomad, Long Poem Magazine, M58, Matthew's House, New Writing, Noon, Otata, Queen Mab's Teahouse, The Quint, Raceme, Rockface* (exhibition, Jam Records, Falmouth), *Ship of Fools, Stride, Tears in the Fence, Third Way, Tract* (Recent Works Press, 2017), *Visitant, X-Peri.*

Thanks to Mike, Peter, Andy, Jane, Sarah, Harvey, Martin and Paul for ongoing poetic support; to Maria Stadnicka and Martin Caseley for help with editing this book; and Tony Frazer for publishing this and my other collections.

Contents

TAKING THINGS APART

The Age of Destruction and Lies 11
About the Sky 12
The World's Oldest Star Map 13
Before it Starts to Rain 15
At This Moment 16
Counsellor and Confidante 19
Common Ground 21
Contradicting Reality 22
Fake Brain Maps 23
Even That 24
Left Behind 25
Home Run 26
How to Dismantle a Sculpture 27
In the Shadows 28

THE SHAPE OF PARADISE

Off to the Future 33
The Only Known Photograph of God 34
God Thoughts 35
Not Here 36
A Theology of Absence 38
Quiet Prayer 40
Religious Futures 42
A Closer Look 44
The Shape of Paradise 45

MATERIAL FORM

Untitled Abstract 49
Look Through Water as We Look Through Air 50
Modernism Is Not Your Friend 51
Postmodernism Is Not Your Friend 52
Surrealism Is Not Your Friend 53
Dada Is Not Your Friend 54
An Interpretation Beyond Understanding 55
Approximately Inbetween 57
Schrödinger's Cat Is Not Your Friend 59
Either a Snarl or a Smile 60

BOMB DAMAGE MAPS

The Lore of the Land 67
Topographies 69
Westway 71
High Rise 73
Catalogue 76
A Windscreen onto the World 78
Underneath 80

MAXIMUM TWITCH

Lines from the Library 85
Email Body Text Table Button Table 86
Mending a Broken 87
Note to Students 88
Note to Self 89
Note to All 90
The Most People 92
Punctuation to Fix 83

The Now Delusion 95
The Ruin of Here 96
On the Way 97
Utopia 99
The Sadness of Things 101

Love to Sue, Natasha and Jessica.

TAKING THINGS APART

The Age of Destruction and Lies

So how do we understand and act upon
the doctrine of the separation of powers?

We may be jealous of those who are dead
but a new orthodoxy suggests that

we may *all* be dead before too long, are
acutely susceptible to the coming epidemic.

The best way to understand anything is to use
the science fiction cliché of global consciousness

as a response to unmentionable goings-on
compounded by the decline of social engineering.

Odds are you are happy with how it's all worked out:
creative destruction is the name of the game.

The ultimate consequence of these upheavals
is a predatory intimacy in response to the unmentionable

and badly written puff pieces which are often a pretext
for vivid set pieces and paid trips to the frozen north.

Let's agree that overall goals are often unattainable.
I am understandably sceptical about doppelgängers

and new ideas which circulate among poets too slow
to notice a whole constellation of books and dreams,

but you don't get to choose who reads you
or who does what with music and words.

About the Sky

I have mirrored your accident
and fallen up the stairs, fallen off
the map. I am mostly in hiding
from imagined enemies and critics
of my own devising. You know
how it is: these thoughts arise
and worm their way in, quickly
becoming facts. Everyone is a poet
now and if they are not they borrow
texts and call them their own,
or sing and dance, seek fame
and a public any way they can.
One learns to tire of audiences
and withdraw, preferring to mail
pamphlets to a group of friends,
as though it were still the seventies.
Back then shops were independent
and sometimes sold small books
on sale or return (usually the latter).
We found our feet underground
and watched as business knocked
us over, told us that our poems
would never sell. Then poetry was
the new rock & roll, then it went
online. Everyone's become a critic
and an expert but no-one wants
to read or think about their work.
Everything is in the moment,
everything is now, then gone.
There's dust on all my books
and people don't believe I can
have possibly read them all.
Today I'm flat on my back,
wondering how I might
write about the sky.

The World's Oldest Star Map

sun disk is now
a landmark universe

known green site
travel by magic

oldest surrounded world
known to map lunar use

ground will move sky
set astronomical time

moon tower words
with crescent between

discover our cosmos
in the time of bronze

hypothetical maps
a conceptual clock

axe symbols appeal
as between arrives

site depiction interpreted
stuck where pain's inlaid

patina stones failed
by impact philosophy

these transit travellers
finding having work

chisel star movement
is beautiful and gold

blue diameter full of
temporarily wide night

a great mysterious
time dated device

linking oldest symbols
to surrounding astronomy

the concept of place
history and time

Before It Starts to Rain

Let me say this, before it starts
to rain: I have a fear of mirrors,
am afloat in a lake of distortion.

I know how strange this sounds
but I am a master of destruction
and music is how I avoid

the cartoon madness I draw
for myself. The flickering images
will not go away, torn pictures

are scattered on the floor until
a time when I will sellotape them
back together, a present for myself,

an aid to regret and self-forgiveness.
The elephant in the room
has taken control of the stereo,

and I am inclined now to silence.
We are all in the same boat,
which we are using as an umbrella

because there is no wind. In fact
nothing floats my boat any more
and I have seen this all before.

I know every secret I ever made,
the then and now is gone, inertia
creeps towards the forgotten answer.

At This Moment

My life is cold, and dark, and dreary;
It rains, and the wind is never weary
—Henry Wadsworth Longfellow, 'The Rainy Day'

1.

Housebound and landlocked, eye to window to rain to leaking gutter and sodden towel in corner of the studio. I would be a sunshine man, sitting in the shade; I would be a fairweather sailor sipping onboard wine and watching others daydream. I would be overgrown and forgotten, knowing she is always right and that there is nothing to be afraid of.

Shallow end, strange cadences, the city of the sun

2.

Owl song, moonrise and low cloud. No more fallen branches but the imprint of the last is still there on the lawn, along with this year's acorns. Even asleep I can hear the rain, can feel the dampness of the air and watch the garden path become a stream and then a waterfall as it descends the concrete steps. I am dreaming summer backwards, afraid to live within these clouds.

Ice of the north, dry sands of the desert, morning still hours away

3.

A rusty future calls, one of decaying metal and rotten, broken boughs, things which this quiet man is not well suited for. This long winter of storms and banter has reduced him to hallucination and frostbite, layers of warm clothing and endless online dreams. Everything happens to me, nothing feels the same, my heart is a twisted oak. The children remind me and then move away. There will be different days.

Muddy water, happy sad, thunderclaps and late night booze

4.

All roads from this village lead only to the next, the paths I've found circle through mud back to where they began. I am better than I used to be at all of this, can't wait for me to get here or for silence to be declared. I sing rain songs and cast spells to ward off infection and pain, am waiting for the miracle I promised myself would be here soon. There must be a way to expand into the universe, however hard I want to be like me.

Teenage wildlife, yellow flowers, evening sky on fire

5.

For the birds, for the children, for the person in your life. For the sake of the planet, for the silent majority, for an undisclosed sum. For the uninitiated, for the first time, for the foreseeable future. For good reason, for the benefit of us all, for the rest of the year. For the best experience, one for all and all for one. For the last time, head for the hills. Thanks for nothing, thanks for the dance, I am out for the count. This is where everything falls apart, where I don't know how to begin or end.

The sunsets are meant for somebody else

6.

Drystone songs and fairweather tunes, cardboard boxes cut down to size and stacked under the skylight's grey. It is just you, just me, and the storm outside, dreaming ourselves back to then. In the glimpses between powercuts I imagine phantoms of the sun. Take all the stars and half-tongue the moon, I have been swallowed by the sea.

Call me Noah, call me Jonah, call me up another time

7.

In and out of the fading light and everywhere I go. A small boat in a week-long storm, an echo of my own devising, a rather soggy scream. On the other side of knowing is a hidden future but the forecast is not good. There are invisible seams in the sky and endless streams on the ground. It is not just winter rain and all these crooked words cannot turn things upside down. These are poems for broken birds and stories for strangers, songs about broken shells and flooded roads. An invocation to the god of dry.

Fluid dynamics, solemn goodbyes, black cat sleeping on our bed

8.

Out of all this blue and water come invisible connections and email blessings, messages made of sellotape and glue. Secrets sent from the white starline bring me back to earth, where it is time to become ocean and turn my inner landscape grey. What do I do with all the sorrys owed to my other selves or with the storm within? From nothing to nowhere, I have found another version of me to inhabit and persuade. It is raining in my house but I now have a time machine.

Land of doubt, liquefied, secret passage into spring

Counsellor and Confidante

We weren't really at the gardening stage,
didn't talk about how wounded we were,
how sometimes a mood could take us.
We didn't know magic was collapsing
and adopted strategies weren't working.
Good liars are canny with their audience
and that relationship is worth considering.
Discussion generally focuses on intention
rather than the role of the listener
but lying is a social act and can create
what is sometimes called the plausible,
can create passion and distress, laughter
and dismay when truth's revealed later on.

From my books I learnt great sadness,
derogatory names and social vividness.
I adopted the use of an ear trumpet,
assumed a limp and spoke out about
filth oozing from the gutters and
the moral decay all around. It's hard
to live an energetic life but I tried,
although I could no longer compose,
write or undertake rambunctious
holiday activities. Sordidly innocent
and deterministically depressed,
I sought solace in educated women
and conversation with elected rulers.

At this point we need to look beyond
our impoverished political landscape
and compensate, reconcile and buy
another drink. This is a founding moment,
we should be more radiant than gloomy

even if we have been beaten up, are so
damaged we are almost no longer human.
I spend my time driving aimlessly around
the ring road, treating life as a journey,
burning intensely with a new hatred
for all authority and those who continue
to use the word 'normal'. Memory is all
about being able to change the past.

Common Ground

We have a fixed body of doctrine,
which focuses on force of recognition
and depends upon heroic revolutionaries

drained of rebellious energy, along with
emotionally charged words and moments
intended to have a profound effect.

Lost almost as soon as it appears,
the marvellous is within everyone's reach,
blending the mystical with the spiritual,

the site of a vision where critical function
gives pause to anyone who feels committed
to any type of esoteric influence.

I am searching for a bit of country
in the city, considering a headlong dive
into group-organized consciousness,

a powerfully convergent aspiration
that feels intuitively off-key:
a strong will does not make life easier.

It is a question of educating people
to spend until everything is lost,
of keeping all the wonder caged.

Contradicting Reality

Your teeth will be my piano,
although difficult to tune,
and I hope you will not sneeze
mid-performance. Forgive me
for not learning how to put up
shelves and cupboards straight,
for not being a good nurse
and for not being a natural
musician. I should have been
a gardener but I hate gardening,
could have been a roaring success
but the audience didn't like me
and I wasn't about to sell out.

Your feet will be my wardrobe.
I will hang my shirts in a sensible
order and fold my jumpers too.
My mother taught me what to do
although I refuse to iron anything
and nothing ever dries when
I hang laundry out on the line.
I should have been sensible and
stayed home, could have sent
a postcard if I had been so inclined
but I didn't want to waste my time.
I had a nice holiday and remained
incommunicado, silent and relaxed.

Your mouth will be an echo chamber
for what I forget, what I need to say.
You will speak for me, alert to
the need for politeness, day-to-day
necessity and discourse. Your back

will be my table, your legs a place
to park the car; if it rains I might
borrow your hair to serve as
an umbrella, your arms and fingers
to telephone a friend. I know how
to keep busy and occupy my time:
playing the impossible piano,
sorting out my clean clothes.

Fake Brain Maps

Small electrical fragments, found in the street,
do not rewire my thoughts. Optical trickery
has brought five faded masterpieces back
to life, but does not make my daily routine
any easier. If you believe what Peter says
the past has been rewritten according to
fugitive and rather lovely principles.
It took a month for the inks to dry
and the scan to be processed but I was
signed off in the end. All clear! Or not so
clear: I can't see where the tumour isn't,
nor where the probes went in. Angels
and devils stay in orbit and out of reach,
all that heaven allows is hot chocolate
and a singsong. Faith is just a sound
in the night, the same rituals re-enacted
time and time again; radio voices mutter
as you play with random images onscreen.
Something has gone horribly wrong,
this story is made up, there is nothing
wrong with me at all; I am merely riding
a wave of discontent and hoping for
better things to come. Editing isn't
an option: compare the restored photos
with the faded paintings on the wall.

Even That

I never liked anything
as much as his first book
and he never liked me
saying that. Later on,
he got serious and it all
went wrong; you can
have too much of
a good thing, even if
your motives make sense.
I must drive to the funeral,
to pay my respects, say
the things I have to say,
mainly hellos and good
-byes. Don't think about
how we are composed,
decomposed or composted,
are all over the place.
I never liked anything
very much but now
even that is gone.

Left Behind

Who is that man who can't remember
how to work the computer, who cried
when he lost his wife? Who forgets
to send the work he has promised
and struggles to speak on the phone.
Not the poet I knew but endless words
which jabber and twist, excitable phrases
collapsed into awkward conversation.

Endless digression brings me back
to the hospital where my father died,
the big house where great aunts and uncles
lived. There used to be an airfield, a mansion
on the corner; you could turn right across
the main road or cycle up the hill to work
with its racing car stored in the warehouse.
The past will not stay away, it returns

in old films, in the notes to the books
you read. It is online, in photo albums
abandoned in my study; it turns up
in letters or phone calls, or you see it
out of the corner of your eye. How long
since we lived there? The past I mean.
It always moves away, leaving us behind.
Things are so unclear when you look aside.

Home Run

'Someone we loved is under this ground so we all come back
  and call it *home*'
    —'Ground', Cecilia Woloch

Someone we loved is under the ground
and one day it will be me, one day it will be you.
I miss us already, am not ready to die.

To me, the glass never looks full, and anyway,
I have a habit of spilling my drink, the boys
will tell you all about it. That and my sneezing;

we don't know if it's chocolate or beer
or perhaps dog hair in the pub. Maybe I'm just
allergic to life, should get ready to move on.

Shaving in the mirror, the new bathroom lights
reveal that my hair is going grey. I don't mind,
it's just I hadn't noticed until now, am surprised.

Summertime ends tonight. I'm glad of the extra hour
but will miss the evening sun, the few moments
in the garden this autumn's warmth and light

has granted me when I'm home in time. I watch
someone else's mother die on television, listen
to the voices of the dead, singing me to sleep.

Someone we loved is under the ground
and one day it will be me, one day it will be you.
I miss us already, will not be racing you to heaven.

How to Dismantle a Sculpture

The sculpture should be dismantled progressively, with every step introducing new components and mechanical connectors which are to be detached from previously built art.

Taking sculptures apart can be fun and a learning experience, as my class found out at a Take It Apart Party. Students found magnets, small speakers, spirals of wire in a cone shape, and lots of soldered pieces inside. Dismantling turned out to be at least as much fun as putting it together.

Offer multi-step dismantling instructions in vector graphic format, grouping the graphic primitives into semantic elements representing individual parts, mechanical connectors (e.g. screws, bolts and hinges), arrows, visual highlights, and numbers.

The order of dismantling is not crucial, but top down is a good way to go. Begin with the easy-to-remove external accessories, using an open-ended wrench to disconnect. If bits do not spring loose easily, give them a gentle tap with a hammer, then lift them clear before abandoning the project.

Loosen all of the bolts and disconnect it from its mount. Push. Apply excessive pressure.

We are taking things apart because we want to.

In the Shadows

Sometimes someone else has to sing the song
before we notice how great it is.
Sometimes a stranger points to a painting
and the whole things comes alive.

Sometimes we go back to the dusty corners
of our lives and excavates the past,
uncovering people and places, happiness
we had chosen to forget.

Sometimes it hurts and we wish we hadn't
but sometimes we need to know
what is hiding in the shadows and why
we chose to put it there.

Sometimes it is unclear, sometimes things
sparkle in today's new light,
sometimes we wrap it up again in newspaper
or an old curtain, return it to the

sometimes we correctly decided
was where it belonged.
Sometimes the corpse in the corner stirs
and the whole thing comes back to life.

THE SHAPE OF PARADISE

Off to the Future

'Take away his camera and he'll draw on
his eyeballs with a felt-tip pen.'
—Iain Sinclair, *The Last of London*

Compulsion and a flying heart. Nothing
will go away, nothing stays the same.
He is behind the curve or ahead of
the game, never quite where he wants
to be. How very sad, how lovely, how
does he manage to cope? Picture this:
animal tracks and bone, black glass,
Sunday morning childhoods. Gone
or tidied up. Memory fades away,
the past is open to interpretation.
The darkness falls as flowers do,
wilting in the light; although we are
earthbound we can't wait to get away.
Don't make me choose, don't make me
explain or err on the side of caution.
I need to see, to undo the damage
and find out everything for myself.
We can argue about the secrets
of the past but I am looking forward,
ready to go yet full of regrets.
Hold my hand and we are off
to the future, walking sideways
and dodging our own reasons
as well as the camera's flash,
mumbling damaged prayers.

The Only Known Photograph of God

'When you get a clearer picture you can understand
why so many want to stand in the dust cloud,
where there is comfort in confusion.'
—Thomas Merton

The only known photograph of God
turns out to be a silhouetted skyhook
slung from a wire, holding nothing
and not moving at all. It is not
uplifting or impressive, the sky
is grey, the image black and white.

What did the monk who took the photo
mean? Was it a surrealist joke or a way
to make an oblique comment about
expectations or absence, the unknown?
He took up meditation, talked in zen
and went to meet the Dalai Lama,

then his maker. Left us notebooks
and a damaged small black painting,
photos and calligraphies, a mystery
shaped hole in the centre of his work.
It is totally absurd to expect answers
that might help explain our world.

God Thoughts

'The poem is a prayer spoken to a God
who only exists while the prayer lasts'
—Eugenio Montejo, 'El Taller Blanco'

The poem took flight and took off for heaven,
where the angry forgotten god was surprised
to receive it; it had been a long time
and email was never quite the same,
especially with a dodgy internet connection.

He didn't want any more hallelujahs, songs,
pleading or special cases, any more sermons
that tried to make people laugh. After all,
it was him who'd created jokes and humour,
and there was nothing left to laugh about.

Everything was spoilt, the poems didn't
even rhyme! Art was just splodges of colour,
vague ideas, or light projected on a wall.
What on earth had he done? The poem
stayed there, getting in the way.

God hated being nagged by words.
They'd bugged him from the beginning,
then teamed up with consciousness
in an attempt to make people think.
He used to know how to walk on water.

Not Here

for David Grubb

And if the god is not here then we must find him
or invent him, make him up and make him stay,
take up residence among the silences, the cold
damp stone and peeling paint. He might not
like it here, of course, but it is our universe
and the god must play by our rules and listen to
our songs, along with the angels on the roof.

And if the god does not like us dreaming him
then he must leave the world and walk away
into the night, leave us in the dark to pray
and wonder where he has gone and where
he might have been before. The blue mountains
are his, and the grey seas, even the small city
where we once lived, this village where we do.

And if the god will not talk to us, then we will
have to shout louder, and argue and plead
and make promises we cannot keep, especially
when we wheedle and whine and make requests
no real god would bother with, what no wise god
would allow us to do. He will not fight our wars,
he will not make us rich, he will not show himself

to us, for if the god is here then we will not
have to find him or invent him, and if we do not
we will never know him for ourselves and if we
do not get to know him then our dreams will be
empty and pointless, and we will never be granted
our wishes and desires, however worthy they are.
And if we cannot get what we want, then we do not

need the god, because that is what we want him for. If he is not here he must be elsewhere, or nowhere, maybe with the angels. The bells crack and clang, our buildings remain empty. It is hard to imagine why we thought we needed the god or could not live without him. He would not like it here even if we could find him or the time to make him up.

A Theology of Absence

'The melancholics concern themselves with the
structure of doubt, rather than the structure of
belief, because doubt is inventive. Doubt complicates.'
—Lisa Robertson, *Nilling*

If we had known where we were going
we might not have gone. 'Paradise'
is mostly beige with yellow stripes
splashed diagonally across the canvas
and light orange hidden underneath.
It is poured and scraped and brushed;
not one of his best. I cannot face
reading any more of my poems
and was disappointed I am not
in the new issue of the magazine.

All night we emailed each other
with strange strings of association
and despair, questions about
whys and whens and wherefores,
ideas of what to listen to next,
ignoring each other's answers.
Insomnia as a creative tool,
a fruitful exercise, not simply
being awake. You questioned
if either of us were actually real;

to be honest, I just don't know.
It would take longer than this
to find out if truth or Truth exists
or are for the knowing, if evolution
and colour, time, or a theology
of absence are worth any more

debate or worry. I am various
and you are concerned. We move
millimetre by millimetre towards
comprehension and deep sleep.

Quiet Prayer

It was not a quiet prayer.
When it came, it was
wrenched from him, in anger
or pain, possibly both, but
it was definitely a shout
not a whisper, was certainly
something directed at god,
certainly heartfelt and
demanding, absolutely sure
of its reasons and concerns.

It was not a quiet prayer,
it was a scream of grief
ripped out of the night,
pain from hearing the worst.
It was primal and personal,
a shout about being alone
and not knowing what to do,
a request for a compass,
a map and survival rations.
But mostly a demand for love.

It was not a quiet prayer
and it whispered its way
around the village, out
into the world. Elsewhere,
on their knees, others
were shocked at the raw
hurt, the need; took prayer
upon themselves, spent time
begging for mercy
and pleading for his soul.

It was not a quiet prayer,
it was prayer nourished
by dissolution and despair,
a loud eccentric mash-up
of energy and anger,
questions and desire,
despair spun loose
into the world to see
where it would go and
if anyone would answer.

Religious Futures

'Let my prayer be set forth before thee as incense;
and the lifting up of my hands as the evening sacrifice.'
—Psalm 141: 2

'Aimed at the peripheral frontiers of the digital world where the young people dwell, the Click To Pray eRosary serves as a technology-based teaching tool to help young people pray the Rosary for peace and to contemplate the Gospel. The project brings together the best of the Church's spiritual tradition and the latest advances of the technological world.'
—*Vatican News*, 15 October 2019

This is an experimental device, a tool for learning how to pray.
The era of invention began and the machine came into being,
a wearable technology bracelet featuring a crucifix interface
with built-in camera, infra-red sensors, microphones,
incomprehensible incantations for deep coma worship.

Electronic rosary machines connect with smartphone apps
for guided prayer and hypnotic communication rituals.
The gadget aims to help the young achieve world peace
and contemplate, practice and propagate the gospel.
The equipment also awards Prayer Bonuses when used.

For aeons, people have reached out to the Almighty
but now you don't have to have his e-mail address
or understand the relationship between structure
and culture or bother with religious demography
and survey results. The future is here right now.

Will our gods die out altogether? Human lives
are cheaper than machines in almost every country
of the world, but everybody still needs systems
and methods for enhancing prayer. We must look
to the past, to founding myths, old religions

and ancestral lines. Our jokes may be bad
but hopefully our content is more informative
than alternative scenarios and final conclusions.
This experimental device is our shared future,
now we should have everything we need.

The music of the prayer machine is constantly purring
through my body. For the most accurate intercessions
it should be kept flat and at a proper distance from
electromagnetic fields, fervour, interfaith communities
and cultural despair. Welcome to the temple of tomorrow.

The essential nature of prayer is a layering of sound
upon sound, controlled by an alchemy very similar to that
which generates worship music. Users can control piety,
dynamism, plurality and multivocality but please note that
salvation is not included in the price of your purchase.

A Closer Look

Eric Pankey, *Dismantling the Angel*

Smoke and fire, ash and fog,
birds flying in formation,
unseen shadows in the night.

Restless poems trace what you saw
out of the corner of your eye
or might have once believed in.

You want to flesh out these stories
but there are too many versions
and more to write about when

you take a closer look. The language
seems to mute you: you are happy
to be quiet and let others speak.

Wind in the attic, distant crows,
soot and dust, animals and angels.
How to put things back together

now words have taken them apart?

The Shape of Paradise

A strange geometry of faith and doubt
defines the ruthless shape of paradise
in our dreams. There is no difference
between dogma and disease
except the degree of distance
from wonder and the watchtowers
whose guards look down upon us.

Feed the hostage and be generous
to yourself: don't ask questions
you can't answer. Noisy days are over
and the morning is waiting; you are
the song and yesterday was the last time
I was in tune with tomorrow. If we are
to return to forever, we must see things

in a different light, should experience,
not watch in disbelief. Wind up
the Gregorian chant machine
and break out the ritual bells:
we are chasing tales and marching
down ghost roads. At the gate
of dreams lies the angelic city,

as if paintings could ever lie.
The door is open but you cannot go in,
for there is more to understand.
I am not who I thought I am
and neither are you. Faint mystery
turns out to be closer to chaos
than the new frontier. Visitors

are turned away, a stranger's horse
is tethered outside, the safety boat
has gone adrift. There is fuzzy logic
at work and the magician in me
has run out of spells. Soft spoken words
will not keep us warm, it is always
winter in heaven and the flesh is weak

with nowhere to go. The god
of ocean tides has gone for a sail,
the crow of shadows and night
has stolen the sun. If we take care
of illusion then the rules of the game
should become known. Facts is facts
and now it's all clear as morning mist.

MATERIAL FORM

Untitled Abstract

smudge of charcoal on the photograph covered her eye.
right-angle wire held up the painted strut. pink and brown
smeared into each other. several dots in several colours
gridded across the small canvas. a simple representation
of leaves. many greys. scribbled lines over a loose yellow
ground. mostly black with a few blue patches. untitled.
white over grey over black over canvas. thin lines of colour.
sprayed red and spattered with pale cream drips. outline
of an imaginary country. charcoal, graphite and pastel
on cream paper. all kinds of blue. several suns and many
squares. careful overlays and the idea of a circle. reds and
purple against the strangest green. ink and pencil. inversed
and dribbling monochrome rainbow. this grey, that grey
and several other greys. orange fire and erased charcoal.
sharp edge of hard colours meeting. soft puddled stains.
primitive figures on graph paper. untitled abstract. trace
elements. I tell myself secrets, offer you painted words.

Look Through Water As We Look Through Air

(Cremona)

A small city full of emptiness, shadow absences in the sun. I follow my nose from church to church, damp frescoes to chipped saints: smoke and wax, electric candles and patterned reliquaries below heavy ceilings. Beyond brick walls, private gardens and tall trees, in the squares dust and benches for us to share. I am lost in sunlight and market debris, in soundscapes and sound worlds, home-made films, pigeon talk and cathedral bells, eurodisco and late night chat.

Clear dark sky sends cool air into my hotel room. Space and time and the visual, Bill Viola's slow-moving figures and the sounds of distance, of silence, the close-miked today; the sounds of steps and voices, cat purrs and paintbrushes, the echoes of a tunnel in time, characters who cannot see each other. Everyone knows someone else we almost know: zoom to rain on the windscreen, pan out to watch the clouds go by.

The market scaffolds itself into being, disappears by afternoon, so what remains can be swept up. Everyday perception is disrupted: five faces in a dark room, digital glitches and delay disrupt our point-of-view. I am above it all, immersed in it all, a visitor frozen in a hotel window, four floors up with no-one in the dark to pray for me.

Is it art or a documentary, a provocation or the avant-garde? What do we gain from drilling down in isolation? I like the shelves of found objects – glass and china, stone debris – in the museum of archaeology. Kingsley climbed the tower past the pendulum, swinging straight as the world turns. Traffic noise fades, frescos change colour, there are no questions from the audience. We are all immersed in sound and sunshine, concentrating on the view outside and the audio-visual equipment's hum.

Modernism Is Not Your Friend

It's difficult to stop thinking about
how it worked and why, how all
the great authors around at that time
knew and influenced each other,
and why their work's so hard to read.

Modernism is not your friend, it makes
up avant-garde ideas and insists upon
experimentation. It wants to grapple
with love and sex, the invention of
time, photography, and ideas of the self.

It's difficult to stop thinking and dream,
to take the subconscious seriously,
turn image into text. Fragmentation
and collage impede the flow of words,
disrupt both description and plot.

Modernism is not your friend, can be
detrimental to your health, sexist, old
and out-of-date. *Ulysses* is only useful
to hold open the door, *The Waste Land*
should be sold off for social housing.

'It is time to resume unfinished business.'

Postmodernism Is Not Your Friend

I don't know what they were thinking about
when they invented the term, I mean
everything went to hell and back, nothing
stable survived, little was left to believe in,
and there was certainly nothing to read.

Postmodernism is not your friend. Complexity
can be *apropos* of emptiness, games become
gobbleydegook. It's clear this was no accident;
there was a huge market-driven cultural shift
and everyone bought damaged goods.

What were they thinking about, the critics
who stopped critiquing and talked about
anything at length? In essays and books
they drew lines between this and that,
hoping it would start to make sense.

Postmodernism is not your friend, pastiche
only wants to be loved. It refuses to argue,
just gently satirizes, knows there is no truth;
wants to unhinge every stable identity,
recompose and reinvent the past.

'But I want to be a household name!'

Surrealism Is Not Your Friend

Behind the thinking, unknown thoughts,
juxtapositions and other meanings.
Ideas take flight and turn into birds,
the clock leaks time and everything
is fluid, wide open to interpretation.

Surrealism is not your friend, it wants
to seduce you into neural dancing,
wants you to believe that what is
secret and hidden is better than
understanding the world around us.

Behind the thinking, unknown thoughts
jostle and argue for attention. We make
up fantastic stories, attribute importance
to what was previously ignored, place
random thoughts in disorganized rows.

Surrealism is not your friend, it wants
to draw lines between unconnected dots,
wants to delve deeper into the sublime,
wants you to come out and play. Overhead,
a man in a hat floats towards the clouds.

'The stars are washing towards us.'

Dada Is Not Your Friend

It does not involve thinking, this
collaged and cut-up text, the rigid
anarchy of process and performance.
Does strategy have any effect
or purpose? Not necessarily.

Dada is not your friend, although
it's much better now. The kite dance
is the past tense, the close of a song
a broken bicycle on the motorway,
which was damaged from the start.

It does not involve thinking, this
way of misdirecting the reader.
So many ambiguities and possibilities,
impossible events and social pressures,
mean there's often a wobble going on.

Dada is not your friend, although
there is room in the tavern of ruin
for us all to touch and seek revenge.
The poem is like a broken mirror,
only reflecting memories back.

'Give thanks for the chance to think.'

An Interpretation Beyond Understanding

We are visibly fading where exposed
to the sun. I have slapped myself
in the mouth with my mobile and still
can't shut up. I like to hear voices

offering an interpretation of the universe
which is beyond understanding; we have
exceeded ourselves to no useful purpose,
given ourselves to an end we're as yet

unfit for. Layers of glass and shades adjust
and direct the light forever if you've got
any sense; too much light can damage
or destroy pigments. Everybody needs

to unbutton, have an uneasy relationship.
Sometimes I think people make things up,
especially words. You do the past and present
as well as the future if you're in the know.

Too much echo, too much up; too much
echo, too much sound; I would really like
to hear voices. Measuring the change
was challenging, the results impressive.

Light can be used to restore the appearance
of lost colour without touching any of
the senses. Optical trickery has brought
five faded masterpieces back to life, an end

we're as yet unfit for. We are visibly fading,
went downhill fast: too much echo, too much
light, and I still can't shut out lost colours
without touching the canvas. I would like

to hear voices but we are sticks and sawdust
stapled to the canvas, echoes in the dark.
I think they call it the Golden Section,
which can't be seen in ordinary light.

Approximately Inbetween

The thin colours and painted veils,
were like layers in the rock,
earth compressed, compounded,
stratified. Greys melded into blue,
covered other greys, allowed a red
to shimmer through. The ocean
and the sun shone in the window,
white walls framed the canvasses
he hung up to view. He could
not name all the shades or tones
of white, of grey, of colours
in between other colours, but
he would try to mix them on
the broken mirror he used
as his palette, learnt to
replicate layers by underpainting,
using collaged card, allowing
glue to spill and dry. The results
were astounding, the work
didn't feel like his. In one way
that was freeing, in another
simply shocking. Was he inspired
or in denial? Was it involuntary?
There were a million colours
he could use and when he did
it was clear he was to blame.
But here, trying to be subtle,
to approximate, learn from,
perhaps even study and copy,
there was a kind of shift away
from self to other, a slippage
toward another sort of inspiration.
He didn't like that word, because

all too often it was an excuse
for lazy thinking, for turning
experience into fiction or poetry,
relying on some idea of *truth*.
You could be true to yourself
by making it up, inventing
a process or letting words
and paint speak for themselves.
He knew he would always be
in the mix, quite liked the idea
of being hidden in the gaps
between or the splashes on
the edge. Let them focus on
the words, the shapes and colours,
anything apart from *story* or *scene*.
Let things be ordered but inconclusive.
He stood back in his studio to look
at the work pinned to the wall,
pretended he was a stranger
attempted to be critical.
The radio talked about nothing,
the rain was still falling outside,
the cat was asleep on the chair.
He wished it wasn't always so.

Schrödinger's Cat Is Not Your Friend

What was Schrödinger thinking? The cat
is actually either dead or alive,
whether or not it has been observed.
What does this famous thought experiment
really mean? Does anybody care?

Schrödinger's cat is not your friend. If he was
he also wouldn't be, would purr and hiss
at the same time, would eat and not eat,
sit in a box and out. He's a flawed
interpretation of quantum superposition.

What was Schrödinger thinking? He was
thinking too much it seems. If only
he'd had a cat it would have calmed him,
distracted him from working, saved him
from answering hypothetical questions.

Schrödinger's cat is not your friend. He wants
to sleep, without poison or geiger counter,
without any theoretical considerations to
consider, no flirtation with the impossible.
Doesn't care or know if he's alive or dead.

'Everything here changes and nothing appears to.'

Either a Snarl or a Smile

A triptych for Francis Bacon

1. Often Disturbing Paintings of the Human Figure

Put together entirely from prefabricated elements,
Bacon's more figurative shadows emerge
nourished by his passion and his despair,
disturbing images of anxiety and alienation
in the heart of his favourite stomping ground.

Grotesquely distorted faces and twisted body parts,
a metaphor for corruption of the human spirit,
capture the abstract forms of trauma and denial,
the intimacy that binds its inhabitants.
Intellectuals really are a hopeless lot.

Visitors to the exhibition were shocked
by the transmission of affect through touch,
the eroticization of the disciplinary gaze,
the absolute power of the forces of the past,
painful beauty, endless boozing and desire.

From global billionaires to *art* market fraud,
the frame of mind of those around us
is a powerful mix of disgust and fascination,
a singularly spastic rebellion where style
is replaced by token visual affinities.

And you, forgotten, memories ravaged
drank everyone else under the table,
synthesized ideas of the harpy, electronics,
skyscraper housing estates, animals and cars,
into a puzzling version of elucidated thought.

Nothing but specialised activities everywhere
dissimulating cacophonic manifestations
of recent revivals of interest, the kind of *art*
that often surfaces into view, unconscious
forces operating beneath an impressive facade.

2. Absolute Mischief

spastic shadows replace the past
global despair's drunk disgust
human passions distort surfaces
thought now memory's metaphor
elements of Bacon's alienation
evidence of conscious mischief
forgotten forms of abstract nothing
body mix and disciplinary surfaces
distorted beneath twisted disgust
favourite memory transmission

faces more than hopeless
images of corruption and history
manifestations of erotic global art
blank forgotten memories replaced
stomping passions disturb despair
hopeless denials elucidate everywhere
past memories prefabricating culture
the human view in abstract surfaces
heart a drunken afterthought
improvised visual cacophony

affinities nourish shadow surfaces
gaze and alienation touch a face
passions twist around smashed coil
faces inhabit forgotten memories

powerful disturbing bodies blend
twisted forms of mischief mix
trauma manifestations of disgust
more ravaged body surfaces
figures shocked by intimacy
distort fraud's culture ground

beauty affects conscious gaze
stomping the disciplinary past
questioning mind forgotten
a puzzle figure once human
transmission touch operating
more stuff made from nothing
conscious ideas bind the grotesque
materials processed to deform
our history replaced entirely
painted beauty in denial

3. A Nothing Box

The pressure of exchange value and technology,
the idea of a self-contained subject,
encircles every form of conditioning;
the flat ground of the background colour
an essential product of the capitalist market.

The frisson to be found in injuries
emphasise sensation redesigned
in accordance with the development
of society as a whole: systematic exclusion
synonymous with utmost extremism.

The present as a historic problem,
reduced to torsos and mutilated heads,

Joe Soap intellectuals, pataphysicians, artists,
crypto-fascists and psychedelic impresarios,
offering us either a snarl or smile.

They look like nothing, foreshadowing
deconsecrated and fragmented myth,
imagery embedded within the origins
of animal and human consciousness,
cultural tradition meshed with cruel desire,

lurid scenes of violence and torture,
maws open as if howling or screaming;
everyone placed under the divine spotlight,
excited crowds watching someone who
has been driven desperate seeking

engagement with the ground, a place
where one makes oneself and a time
in which one plays: scrubby grassland,
blue ground smeared with a green tinge,
devoid of visible human occupation.

God was the guarantor of space and time,
a brilliant stage manager, not an original artist.
The end of all values is a nothing box,
a duet of paint upon paint.
You even get to like it in the end.

BOMB DAMAGE MAPS

West London Blues

The Lore of the Land

On other occasions the people did
convince themselves of intentions
to uprise and take back control
but apathy and commonsense
soon sent them back to work,
to daily routines, to shop, to bed.
Each day went much as before;
is a tradition among inhabitants
to do so. Is a blessing and a boon.

On one occasion the car was towed
to an unknown garage. Was never
recovered or repaired, though always
had an MOT, bought round the corner
from where he used to live. *Win a trip
to NYC* said the chocolate biscuits
wrapper he couldn't afford, *Tories
out* said the wall and the gossip
in the pub. But they wouldn't go.

South of the village is an intersection,
and storytellers agree that questions
must remain unanswered. The book
is a magic ritual, maintained to be
written by the natives. Sickening
is not allowed, of neither the heart
or the body. All must be restored
by unknown powers and you must
show you are available for work.

Traditionally, ghosts are associated
with the past, what went before,
but others call this idle fiction.

Reformation and revolt is often
punished and misunderstood
by other generations. Condemned,
we ride through implications
and denial, accused of sorcery.
Questions remain unanswered,

answers remain unattached. Let
the show continue, let bygones
be history and history be gone.
Let us commence, let us be lovers,
let us in or out, just let it drop.
Legends about the city abound.
No son of mine will ever die
by drowning, I own my luck and
each day happens much as before.

It is said tradition only speaks
when spoken to, and speculates
that it ceased and was filled in.
The screams of a woman haunt
this place and the king and all
his army became stones. Which
tree is meant is unclear, as no-one
will own the watch. But all agree
what this is is not said or known.

Topographies

She made a suit made of maps,
made a dress made of maps,
papered her kitchen with maps.
She was going nowhere but
she could dream. And did.

Made a map made of maps,
a world to get lost in, a world
of impossibilities and broken
mountains, roads and streams.
When I reach this place I will stop.

Walked in shoes pasted over
with maps. Host in her hive,
guide to her own inclusive holiday.
Made her son's football into
an abstract globe, all ocean

and land, and then another.
Papered chairs and the table,
doors and windows, blinds
a squiggle of roads and lanes
all leading to her backyard.

The map as an image is
a popular form of decoration,
thereby showing its qualities as
substitute for travels as well as
a means of orientation.

Made a map made of maps,
all borrowed mountains and hills,
blues and greens, red lines,

a public house by the stream.
She owned no right of way,

was no safe passage marked
across her land. Imagine being
lost everywhere, imagine quitting
in the middle of a tour. She paced
round her garden then went inside.

Westway

See the scars beside the concrete
where houses used to be, people
used to be. A horse in a dried-up
muddy field, graffiti for company:
Where is your god now? a dripping
question that can't be answered.

Painted the scene purple and gold
but couldn't hide the damage. Cars
drove faster to get to nowhere quicker
than they ever had. A skatepark
sprang up and splintered, the gypsies
moved on, leaving a scrapyard behind.
The tube offers the best view: squint left
and imagine a neighbourhood divided
by demolition and elevated road. Imagine
a riot on your hands, a fire 24 stories tall
and next door dying or gone missing.

Where is your god now? He is a row
of concrete statues holding up the road,
is a horse remembering grassier days,
is speculation all, no material evidence.
Is working for human rights groups,
is plotting the ley lines that gather here,
is looking for his name in the phonebook,
is probably a prince looking for a princess,
is too old to move away now. Is stuck,
is buried in the cellar, is underneath
the arches, is pouring cold water
on all his own ideas. Is forgotten.

Is Saturday morning in the market,
the discarded is being repurposed,

the freeway connection ignored.
Jazz and reggae lubricate damp clothing
and stale smoke, everything is cheap
or overpriced. There's nothing I want
but it is somewhere to be, something
to do, is a diversion from the rest
of the week, is a diversion: you must
turn left, follow the yellow signs until
they stop and you is lost. (Rumours
that ghosts are to be seen walking.)

Is years later and nothing has changed
although traffic jam above is longer
and slower. Is a shopping centre nearby
and an encampment of homeless men
living in plastic and cardboard. Is
a desultory space, curving shapes
divide sky and landscape in visually
arresting ways. Is private and is public,
is glimpsed from the train, is whiplash
and shadow, sounds of purpose up above.

Is two chairs and an upturned crate
around a fireplace made of stones.
Is signs of habitation, desolation,
abandonment and discard, is home
to no-one anyone knows. There used
to be a second burial chamber
in a field not far away, used to be
a jumble of boulders, was once
a church on a hill here, houses
where people would eat and sleep.
Now is only grim skyline, cold ash,
the great round eyes of stray dogs,
next day happening much as before.

High Rise

24 floors of incendiary backfire,
flames reforming the sky, sirens
for miles around, repercussions
for years to come. Most local
tower blocks are not yet safe,
is money to be made elsewhere.
Is not a priority, accommodation
will be made available as and when.

Life on the never-never is not
enough. There is not a dry eye
in the house, there is not a floor
left habitable, there is nothing
to be done. Nature as divine entity
is part of our relentless desire
to classify, label and ~~burn~~ know.
Each person's narrative is still
their own, but they own nothing
else, live at the edge of negative
space and grief, poverty and guilt,
with the lingering smell of fire.

Everything is subtly blurred
and discarded. Lives taken away
in skips, a tower block dressed
in green beside the motorway
into town. Gawping drivers
and old news, a charitable fund
and lost neighbours. Other
variables are in play, emotions
run high, trains run late.

Not an attempt to understand,
is sound given shape to words,
distant observations from the
train ride into town. I live
in the suburbs, haven't had time
to look into these things
or become a misery tourist.

24 floors that could have been
saved, 24 floors that are too high
for normal habitation. They are
building 44 floors nearby:
scratch the sky, hope no-one
has vertigo or drops a match.
Will not be clad with same,
will meet health and safety
regulations, will cost more
than risk and death can justify.

Bomb damage maps show what
is missing and what is at risk.
Areas destroyed, areas of fire,
areas where it is not safe to live.
But there is nowhere else to go.
Grief and rage mark anniversary,
72 people died, ~~you~~ we are doing
almost nothing. Put your trust
in anger, in official inquiry,
in a black sack over there.

A wall and barbed wire fence
separates towpath from
an area under the road,
but local legends are made
from cultural ragbag, fleeter

than wind and faster than fire.
Next time, you should and must
link up with the neighbours,
form one massive community.

Council housing blocks around
the church were adorned with
green scarves and the nave was
packed with people wearing
the same colour, holding up
pictures of loved ones they lost
and carrying white roses to lay
later at the base of the tower.

Catalogue

I bought the book because of memory,
not because of art. Paintings retain
an appearance of speed, spontaneity
and freshness, vital satisfactions
I depend upon to navigate my past.

Major creative uncertainties are said
to have been founded by an otherwise
unknown saint, a plucky little survivor
in the shadow of the concrete monolith,
trying to be heard above traffic's roar.

A fenced off and graffiti-strewn area
is the most common item of village
mythology. Arise and march on to
victory or the local on the corner.
The official enquiry is still going on.

A ghost used to be seen here, legend
has it that he was a wizard or a tramp,
maybe the disputed site of a church,
a mighty tower reaching to the sun
and a road where lorries could race

across the aimless landscape beneath.
Over two miles of elevated motorway,
sliproad crossing the railway, two stubs
on the north side built for connection to
the planned line of an imaginary route.

Strange creatures inhabit this underworld,
bodies buried in the motorway walk
the streets and tell stories, sing songs,

and a local tradition has grown up.
Ask anyone who knows, they'll tell.

Attempts have been made to regenerate
once-abandoned land, to brighten up
the front cover of the official report.
The future requires substantial demolition,
but there will be no compensation.

A Windscreen on to the World

The dank chambers of an underground resting place for London's dead might not look it, but this flyover was built out of a respect, a way of escaping the unkempt, swampy cemeteries that were overloaded with bodies from the cholera outbreak. The roads are rarely open to the public, save for occasional tours. Remember, it's an arterial route, not an old railway line.

There are uncorroborated whisperings of a skeleton fully dressed in 1960s finery, with one of the road's spurs named after him and some of his weapons. The locals will tell you that. His ghost can supposedly be seen wandering the tarmac. Other dead dwellers include a shared love interest and the ghost of an unidentified lady wearing white.

Bottled human foetuses, preserved monkey heads and misshapen skeletons are some of the creepy specimens collected for ergonomic research – and all are on display here, or will be when the road re-opens. If deformed bodies and organs don't scare you, then electric lights, hydraulic lifts and air conditioning still pulls fans in from around the world. The A40(M) is the hub of all activity.

Other ghosts have been seen roaming the Western Avenue extension. It might look pleasant enough, but Westway is a 2.5 mile scar with a horrific history. The elevated section connects the mutilated body of a society beauty – limbs strewn under the flyover at ground level – with displays of old surgical equipment, marble heads and dusty documents. The real attraction here though is two giant murals by an artist, just above a forgotten slip road. Apparently, he was so pissed off about the planning he painted these faded stories for free.

You might not be able to hear over the sound of traffic, but a little girl has been reported to weep, slam doors and run along the fast lane, overtaking drivers as they travel. Since the mid 1970s locals have complained about a brilliant orange light emanating from the concrete freeway system. It is enough to give you chills if you find yourself in the aftermath of punk, accompanied only by the echoing footsteps of London and the drip-drip-drip of a leaky sky.

What a great collection of semi-deserted open spaces! Abandoned railway land around the Westway now promotes raw urban ambience but Portobello is lush with vivid greenery although there is still something unsettling about wandering along overgrown cuttings to urban development sites rich in graffiti. It's a little on the haunted side: bleak winter nights in November, London leaps off the balcony of the modern city to find a temporary home out beyond Paddington. Westway marked the beginning of the end.

Underneath

At the end of things, death of course,
and underneath the shake of the traffic
and leftover violence, racist abuse and
things no-one would say out loud
written on the wall, offering new
perspectives on how to navigate
the surface of the city, teaching us
what people really think, why they
won't look us in the eye. This is not
abstraction, is not human perception,
is hatred, cultural war. Properties
of light do not spill down the steps
or ramps, the surveillance cameras
are bust. Everything's slightly blurry,
exaggerates the visual sensitivity
of sore eyes after a full day's work.
The city is not blank or flat: paint
and pencil, rain and weather, mark
and maim, move on to elsewhere.
Is all physiological, all contours
and edges, more than sum of parts.

Eye always looks for boundaries, you
are pushing yours. Where to discover
next? What can you say to inflame
situation that can be passed off as
a joke? Text and image, symbols
and signs: make a mark, move on.
Violence and passion, desire and fear
of everything you're not. Bitten nails,
dirty jeans, tattoos on your knuckles
and a future you forgot. But is not
just clichés like you, is parents,

teachers, friends you might think
better of. All want us to go home.
We shan't. Will stand all night until
time comes to the rescue, have no
other home but here. Will walk nine
times round the open fire, then lay
my head on the turf. There are both
women and men among us, we are
a living company and will be here
as long as it takes us to die.

MAXIMUM TWITCH

Lines from the Library

The poems were configured for maximum twitch,
words threaded together with forward slashes.

Any dancing led to spasmodic jerks at most;
readers simply going through the motions.

I was advised to wear good shoes or go barefoot,
travel cross country and keep two metres apart.

Tomorrow will never be the same again:
into the back silence melt.

Email Body Text Table Button Table

You're talking about the three buttons at the bottom.
If you look at the styles you have, you want the link
to jump to a new workbook and make it entirely clickable.

Select the piece of text you want to send and use columns
and rows to create cells which can contain text or images.
If everything looks good, you can achieve the perfect client.

Paste in content and put their data to good use automatically.
Send it to server via Ajax, send it in person with flowers
and allow users with permissions to access the source.

Optimise for sloppy swiping; references can be ignored,
vertical space should be optimised for artisan migration.
Remember to tell people what your poems are about.

Mending a Broken

'How do you mend a broken etcetera?'
—Dean Young, 'Not Trying to Win No Prizes'

First you make sure the battery
isn't flat, check there is petrol
in the tank and that you have read
the instruction manual. Then you
wind the key, take off the brake
and press the button down:
it should move or turn at once.
If it doesn't then repeat above
and when you are in a bad mood
call the plumber, electrician, mechanic,
and go and do something else.
Make do with candles and your bike,
perhaps shake it gently or bang
the sides, plug and unplug it
several times. Shout at it
then swear. Get it off your chest
and wear something else today.
Whatever you do, keep all packaging,
file the receipt and do not buy
extended warranties or insurance,
simmer gently and then boil
before allowing it to rest. When
you're calm, do more of the same.
Etcetera, etcetera, etcetera.

Note to Students

When I do not give you straight answers
you are confused, when you have to think
for yourselves you are cross. We are not
in agreement about how to learn or why
we are here in this room. You have not done
any preparatory reading but are prepared
to pretend and give discussion a go.
And you would like to blame your phone
along with the college computers
for not printing out what you need.
No-one wants to research a subject,
everyone asks what they actually need
to know, and do not like it when I say
'depends'. But it does and always will,
will always depend on what you want
to say, to do, and who you know, how
you spend your time and if you asked
or are about to ask the right questions,
have begun to think for yourself. It is not
easy learning how to learn, but if you can
life gets easier. There are no exams
to revise for, no tick boxes, and no lists
of facts, you just need to argue and wonder,
to embrace and value confusion.
There will always be too much to read.

Note to Self

Remember there is a narrator
in the poem, as well as an author,
that stanzas do not have to be even
and you can end with a half-line.
Resist the urge to tidy up,
a little sprawl intrigues the reader
and holds their attention as
they navigate the words
laid out on the page. There are
still colours in the darkness,
but they take some searching for.
When I first read Dean Young
I was on a New York hotel bed.
'Listen to these,' I said to Neil
and read several poems out loud.
I did not want, still do not want,
to call it surrealism, there is
more reason and connectivity
than juxtaposition and products
of the subconscious suggest,
but perhaps I am confusing it
with Dada or the idea of chance.
You can see colours in the darkness
but only if you persevere, force
your eyes open and look. I sat
in the Ad Reinhardt retrospective
and stared until his black paintings
went blue, then red: dark squares
with fuzzy edges. And then I sat
and watched other visitors walk
straight through, not choosing
to engage. How I willed them to,
although I must remember there
is an author as well as the self,
a narrator as well as the I.

Note to All

Remember it used to be better,
when we were younger, before it began
to get worse, before it got to this point.
I never asked anyone about the meaning
of life, but probably should have, it's
too late now, they're dead, all information
lost. Trace material and knowledge
slowly fade and disappear, books
go out of print and no-one listens
to those records anymore. As we age
we turn nostalgic, as we turn nostalgic
the past becomes a better place,
our future something we must try
to avoid. Time travel is wonderful:
everything has a rosy glow, everything
we thought was gone comes back,
the people we miss say hi, we get
another chance to make amends
and do things right; well, only in
our dreams. Back in the real world
it's raining, the roads are flooded,
the train tracks under water, and
hardly any students made it in.

I'd like to go home and hug the cat,
read, watch TV or the rain. Damp
shoes and socks, wet hats and coats,
make seminar rooms smell funny;
and my desktop computer is dead.
The beautiful sky will not be back,
sunshine belongs to the past;
it is time for the seasons to change
all over again. How will things evolve?

What will the future involve? And how
will you navigate our legacy, the rubbish
piled high and a world led by leaders
who believe in greed? Jessica says
she will buy a canal boat or campervan,
Natasha a much smaller house abroad,
but they may not have enough money
or permission to travel, now we have
stopped talking to our neighbour states
and each other. We hope it will change
for the better, become like we wanted
it to be, but that seems highly unlikely.
Dark energy is two-thirds of everything
and we still have no idea what it is.

The Most People

In the book I am reading,
a girl turns terrorist
and her mother flees
to South America
to hide and mourn,
run away from herself.
Guilt is scratched
into her every speech,
the kind of nonsense
crowds of strangers
or acquaintances produce,
but her stories change,
as do the names of the people
no-one she talks to knows.
She fills a void with chit-chat
that cannot stop the bomb
exploding with her daughter,
who made it and took it
to where the most people
would die. And they did
and the talking goes on,
not covering up the blood
or screams, the photos
shown on the news
we watched earlier tonight.

Punctuation to Fix

for Martin

I have punctuation to fix, and miles
and miles to go before I drink. Imaginary
escapades and propping up the empty bar
at small press fairs are not what we had
in mind. I have never met a normal poet
yet I find myself attracted to pamphlets
and chapbooks, obscure American imports
and the utterances of writers from small
European states, and others who clearly
cannot write. I often introduce myself
to editors who do not expect me there;
they are always surprised to see me
and I enjoy watching them wriggle
in discomfort and find an excuse
to leave. Trickle-down poetics is
an ingenious idea but all too often
it is only spittle and spilt beer,
for nothing puts off an audience
like a bearded poetry reading
or a glamorous emotional outing
by a well-meaning young woman
or fashionable comedienne. Is that
even a word any more? Is the pope
a bear in the woods? Who would dare
to start a poetry press in this day
and age? Our business model is
a long tail of bullshit, lies and
shouted rhymes that pile up in
the inbox. We can't face reading
and rejecting them. *I'm sorry but*
we are no longer accepting submissions,
says our out-of-office reply. We'll invite

friends and the famous to give us work
for free. Dangle the carrot of publication
and all the donkeys will rush to
your end of the field, hee-hawing
and waggling their poetic ears.

The Now Delusion

'So do we really need to mourn time's passing?'
—Michael Slezak, *New Scientist*, 2 Nov 2013

We might think of time flowing from a real past
into a not-yet-read future but the idea that
time flows past you is just as absurd as

the suggestion that space-time is warped
by the presence of matter to produce
the force we call gravity on a surface

we call the present, shimmering into existence
one moment at a time. You might not be able
to determine what's on the other side,

two events that are both now to you will happen
at different times for anyone moving at
a different speed; the result is a picture known.

Fantastical as it seems, there are things that are
closer to you and things that are further away.
When you gaze down upon the universe,

the only things that are real are language
and moving backwards into the future
with no clear view of where we are heading.

If we gather enough data we will still disagree
on what is happening; there are still wrinkles
that might seem like a zero-sum game

but the prize on offer is a better understanding
of experience in a universe like ours. We are only
ever likely to have a clear backwards view.

The Ruin of Here

'the future is a monotonous instrument'
—Francis Picabia, 'Blind Man's Bluff'

But we still want to get there,
try to climb the stairs too early,
reach the lighted birds, escape
the ruined castles of our lives.

It looks as though they are flying
but it is only projected shadows
on the bare stone walls. It seems
there is a way out but there isn't:

these earth steps will crumble,
turn the power off and the light
will fade. We are not suited
to the dereliction of today.

On the Way

'We enjoy the fiction of encounters, their meaning in the margins'
—Ian Seed, 'Vein'

I am in Santiago, I am in Cremona,
in Samarkand and other places too.
I slip from page to page to country
via an unfocused torrent of poems
and serendipitous reading. Summer
has been and gone but at least I am
back in contact with Mike and Maria,
and poems are starting to leak out
of my computer and nearby printer.

I am going to get a haircut and must
remember to wear aftershave so that
I smell nice for Monday's conference
call. We will have to listen and not
talk, can turn off the camera, drink
coffee in our pyjamas if we wish,
as long as we turn up. Ian's poems
flow everywhere and anywhere,
tracing tributaries and streams,
diverting around people we meet
on the way, pausing to take in
what is written in a notebook or
spraypainted on the wall. There
is nothing can not be in a poem,
nowhere I cannot go if I relax
into my bath with a good book.

If Spain and Italy are out of reach
and I don't dig archaeology then
new poetry criticism offers me

the chance to think about what
Allen wrote, how and why he did.
Maria's draft gongs sound like
a klaxon, disturb my morning,
but with a little editing they ring
and shimmer, conjure sunshine
from the rain. Alistair emails
to give me a link to photos
of missing buildings, it seems
we are all wandering online
looking at what's no longer there.

What isn't there often seems
better than what is. The marks
of demolition, history, fiction,
excite more than the actuality
of the place where we now live.
How quickly we forget to visit
the dissenters' graveyard or walk
past the cathedral; the town
becomes car parks and shops,
just somewhere else to go,
another way to pass the time.

Utopia

It wasn't as dull as she remembers.
We did not sit around in silence,
we went for drinks, riverside walks,
sometimes early morning swims
in the local council pool. We might
have scrubbed up nice for church
but it wasn't all grim silences
or chaste remarks. The world
was breaking up and family, school
and city were each part of that.

Revolution was in the air,
although I was too young to know
that at the time. I was a teenager
who watched huddles of hippies
in the corners of Notting Hill pubs,
rock mutating into punk, the bangs
and whistles, textures and tones,
of carefully improvised noise
played in damp grey rooms
near the railway in Camden Town.

I asked the security guards
to turn the lights on, so we
could look at Ivon Hitchens' mural
of dance and song, found my way
up to the borders of Hampstead
but never went back again.
My patch was further West, where
there were concrete flyovers
and busy roads, a small park
with swings and football pitches.

We made dens on scrap ground,
wobbly platforms of wooden pallets
tied into trees, and cycled everywhere.
Later, bikes became motorbikes
and the city opened up. It wasn't far
up town, and skateboard parks
out East were possible, if you didn't
mind the drive or distrusting looks
from locals. You could park anywhere
and walk into other worlds, could

hear music everywhere, and find out
other words for states of mind
and girls. Scuzzy bookshops sold
secondhand books, science fiction,
experimental novels, strange poetry
and countercultural zines. Friends
who thought the world would change
were everywhere but then started
to disappear. Book and record shops
closed down, it wasn't easy to see

new bands, the basement full of
LPs you could take a 10p punt on
was no more. Everything became
'antique', 'collectable' or 'rare',
as hippies went into business
or moved abroad, having had
enough. Utopia never happened,
its prophets scattered in the sun,
with their confused memories
and straggling unkempt beards.

The Sadness of Things

The sarcasm of birds:
two crows bickering on the empty bird table.

The disappointment of biscuits:
too sweet and crumbly for middle-age.

The distraction of other things:
screens flickering, new music demanding attention.

The disintegration of light:
darkness reflected in a discoloured mirror.

The enigma of memory:
what I remember, what I choose to forget.

The destruction of history:
ancient monuments deliberately reduced to dust.

The seduction of the unknown
rather than what we should care for and love.

The impossibility of calm
and quiet and order, of making a perfect home.

The absence of speech:
words unrecognisable, books left out in the rain.

The elusiveness of meaning:
playful disjunction is not the same as synchronicity.

The sarcasm of birds,
their caws and cries waking me up too soon.

The drawn-out day:
silences, pauses, worry and dismay.

The fickleness of language,
refusing to mean what I want to say.

www.ingramcontent.com/pod-product-compliance
Ingram Content Group UK Ltd.
Pitfield, Milton Keynes, MK11 3LW, UK
UKHW041851190726
13854UKWH00002B/834

9 781848 618893